Thai traditional home cooking series
Volume 1

Classic Thai Stir Fry Dishes

49 kitchen tested recipes you can cook at home

A Thaifoodmaster Ultimate Thai cookbook series

This book is intended to teach you the basics of stir fry cooking:
it will allow you to produce some of Thailand's most popular -
and extremely tasty - stir fry dishes.

TABLE OF CONTENTS

INTRODUCTION

Wok stir frying is a fast, exciting and energetic cooking technique that is absolutely perfect for preparing a tasty meal quickly. Stir frying is an ancient Chinese technique adapted by the Thai people to create an array of delicious favorites that can be enjoyed at home, in restaurants or in the context of speedy à la carte street food.

This book is intended to teach you the basics of stir fry cooking: it will allow you to produce some of Thailand's most popular - and extremely tasty - stir fry dishes.

Wok cooking offers a unique flavor and distinctive qualities: the fast and furious heat - the short cooking time - allow meats and vegetables to cook quickly, preserving their shape, texture, color and nutritional benefits. The round shape of the wok, along with the heat source and its direction, influence the distribution of liquids in the cooking space, as well as the creation of steam and particle-rich vapors that give the food its exceptional taste.

Wok stir frying is not difficult, but there are critical points that should be heeded. A dish's ingredients must be assembled beforehand, and ready for wok cooking action; everything, including the seasoning, must be prepared in advance. The cooking itself is very fast and very immediate, with no single step taking more than two to three minutes.

Choose a good quality wok: one made out of cast iron or carbon steel; or a handmade wok forged and raised, cast or stamped. The wok's walls should be thin to allow fast heat conduction. A thick-walled wok will take longer both to heat up and to release the heat. Wok bottoms should be round, so the liquids will flow and concentrate at the bottom of the wok, where the heat is at its maximum. The main purpose of the heat is to drive out liquids and steam; as water starts to accumulate and boil, it lowers the wok temperature to that of boiling water. Therefore, overloading the wok will fail to produce typical stir fry characteristics: too much liquid will be generated and, without any way to escape, the food will be braised rather than stir-fried. The end result, of course, will be less appealing. The meat will turn tough and the vegetables will be soggy.

Thus, when stir frying anything you want to ensure that you heat the proper-sized wok over a high flame and charge it well with heat. "Proper-sized' refers to a wok of a size that permits you to stir fry the ingredients without overfilling the wok. In home setups this probably means the capability to stir fry a maximum of one or two servings at a time.

Whatever your heat source, it is crucial to have the wok well-seasoned, and nice and hot before adding the oil. This will enable the wok to produce a patina or a nonstick layer, and will prevent food from sticking to the wok. In general, you want to work fast with high heat; however, you may lower the heat and adjust the speed of the cooking depending on the ingredients you use. It's not "one heat level fits all".

Use a high smoke-point cooking oil with a natural taste; for example, canola oil or grape seed oil. You don't want to stir fry with a low smoke-point cooking oil such as a cold-pressed olive oil. Also, strongly flavored oils such as peanut or coconut oil are not common in the Thai kitchen.

Stir fry using a ladle quickly, but gently, toss the ingredients in the wok. This action should move the food away from the bottom of the wok, pushing it to the sides of the wok without breaking it. This will also allow the food to mix with the steam and vapors that are being released. The steam helps the cooking process, and the particle-charged vapors add flavor to the food. Don't simply agitate the ingredients from right to left but, rather, try to move them away from the bottom of the wok. If you can, flip the ingredients by lifting the wok in one hand and tilting the food using round wok movements - that is, moving the wok down and forward, and then pulling back. Be sure that you don't remove the wok from the heat for too long, as you want to maintain a high temperature.

From time to time, it is customary to sprinkle water into the hot wok; it evaporates immediately and this practice serves to deglaze the wok, as well as to release any flavors stuck to the sides of the wok back into the bottom of the wok. Sprinkling water also produces steam that helps in the cooking process.

When the time comes to add the seasoning, make it a habit to pour any seasoning down the sides of the wok, rather than on the food itself; this allows the seasoning to heat up as it reaches the bottom of the wok.

When acquiring a new wok, it is important to season it before using it. The seasoning process creates a thin layer, a patina that protects the wok from rusting and prevents the food from sticking to the wok. Seasoning is accomplished by rubbing the wok with oil and heating it beyond the smoking point of the oil. The heat induces a chemical reaction called "radical fat polymerization", in which chemicals released from the oil crosslink to form a tough film-like coating that adheres to the wok.

To start seasoning a new wok, first wash your new wok thoroughly. Avoid at this time – or at any time in the future - using rough cleaning pads or anything else that can scratch the surface of the wok. Place the empty wok over high heat for about 20 minutes. This will burn off any rust coating that may have been generated by the manufacturer; it will also create toxic vapors, so make sure your kitchen is well-ventilated. As the wok heats up, it will gradually turn grayish-purplish in color. Once the entire surface of the wok has changed color, turn off the heat and let the wok cool down.

The second stage of seasoning is rubbing a thick layer of high smoke-point cooking oil on the inside of the wok, and heating it until it smokes: this is what actually creates the thin protective layer on the wok. When the wok cools down, wipe it with a clean cloth or a paper towel. You should repeat this stage of seasoning each time you use your wok.

A 14-inch wok is a good choice for most home setups. A larger wok requires an intense heat source that is usually unavailable in most home kitchens. A smaller wok is unlikely to accommodate all the ingredients comfortably.

A wok with a wood handle on one side and a small looped handle on the opposite side is the easiest to handle during stir frying, as well as when lifting the wok off the stove afterwards.

RECIPES

Bangkok 1989 -
Not necessarily a woman I knew well, but a woman I knew - a story
about betrayal and disappointments. She used to own a restaurant, a
very good one, that catered to locals and a montage of confused identi-
ties; she used to have a husband; and she used to be the center piece in a
parade of the bizarre. A woman - both charming and mean. I still smile
when I think of her - this portrait of mixed feeling

Bangkok 1989 -
The market of the old neighborhood - the familiar, the worn and usual on a hot night in a ragged, unfashionable part of town - my neighborhood. The smell of cooking food and the glare of florescent lights - and something I miss, now that I've all but forgotten the hard times.

ผัดกะเพราหมูสับ

phat gra phrao muu sap

STIR-FRIED MINCED PORK WITH HOLY BASIL

INGREDIENTS:

200 gr minced pork
1 1/2 tablespoons garlic
1 1/2 tablespoons (or more) red and green bird's eye chilies
1 cup holy basil leaves
1/2 teaspoon dark soy sauce
1 tablespoon natural taste oil

Season with:
1 tablespoon light soy sauce
3/4 tablespoon oyster sauce
1/4 teaspoon ground white pepper
pinch of salt
pinch of sugar
3 tablespoons stock or water

DIRECTIONS:

In a pestle and mortar, roughly crush the garlic. Add the bird's eye chilies; pound together until all the chilies are bruised. Set aside.

Mix all the seasoning ingredients and set them aside.

Place a well-seasoned wok over medium-high heat.

When the wok is hot, pour in the oil followed by the garlic and chilies mixture. Stir fry quickly until fragrant; do not allow the garlic to brown.

Add the minced pork and quickly stir fry, breaking down all the lumps. Continue stir frying the meat until all the liquids have completely evaporated, and the meat dries up and start to brown.

Sprinkle dark soy sauce over the meat and stir fry until the meat turns a nice dark color.

Add the seasoning sauce. Mix together and wait for the sauce to thicken.

Turn off the heat and add the holy basil leaves. Incorporate the basil leaves into the dish using only the residual heat: cooking the basil leaves will cause them to turn black, and will also impair the flavor of the dish.

ผัดกะเพราหมูสับ
phat gra phrao muu sap

ผัดกะเพราหมูสับใส่ขมิ้น

phat gra phrao muu sap sai kha min

STIR-FRIED MINCED PORK WITH TURMERIC AND HOLY BASIL

INGREDIENTS:

200 gr minced pork
1/4 cup yardlong beans, thinly sliced
1 tablespoon fresh yellow chilies, cut into thin strips
1 cup holy basil leaves
2 tablespoons natural taste oil

Chili paste:
1/2 tablespoon fresh turmeric
1/2 tablespoon fresh galangal
2 tablespoons garlic
1 tablespoon (or more) red and green bird's eye chilies

Season with:
1 tablespoon light soy sauce
3/4 tablespoon oyster sauce
1/4 teaspoon ground white pepper
pinch of salt
pinch of sugar
3 tablespoons stock or water

DIRECTIONS:

In a pestle and mortar, pound the fresh turmeric and galangal until smooth. Add the garlic and bird's eye chilies; pound together until the garlic is roughly crushed, and all the chilies are bruised. Set aside.

Mix all the seasoning ingredients; set aside.

Place a well-seasoned wok over medium-high heat. When the wok is hot, pour in the oil, followed by the garlic-chili paste. Stir fry quickly until fragrant; do not allow the paste to brown.

Add the minced pork and quickly stir fry, breaking down all the lumps. Keep stir frying the meat until any liquids evaporate completely, and the meat dries up and starts to brown.

Add the yardlong beans and the yellow chilies. Sprinkle some water to deglaze the wok and create steam.

Add the seasoning sauce, mix, and wait for the sauce to thicken, then add more water or stock as required.

Turn off the heat and add the holy basil leaves. Incorporate the basil leaves into the dish using only the residual heat: cooking the basil leaves will cause them to turn black, and will also impair the flavor of the dish.

ผัดกะเพราหมูสับใส่ขมิ้น
phat gra phrao muu sap sai kha min

เนื้อปูผัดกะเพรา

neuua bpuu phat gra phrao

STIR-FRIED CRAB MEAT WITH HOLY BASIL

INGREDIENTS:

300 gr steamed crab meat
1 1/2 tablespoons garlic
1 1/2 tablespoons (or more) red and green bird's eye chilies
1 cup holy basil leaves
1 tablespoon natural taste oil

Season with:
1 tablespoon light soy sauce
1 tablespoon oyster sauce
1/4 teaspoon ground white pepper
pinch of salt
pinch of sugar
1/3 cup stock or water

DIRECTIONS:

In a pestle and mortar, roughly crush the garlic. Add the bird's eye chilies and pound together until all the chilies are bruised; set aside.

Mix all the seasoning ingredients and set them aside.

Place a well-seasoned wok over medium-high heat, and when the wok is hot, pour in the oil, and then the garlic and chilies mixture.

Sprinkle some water into the wok to deglaze it, then add the seasoning sauce. Mix together and wait for the sauce to come to a boil; add more water or stock as required.

Add the sliced steamed crab meat and quickly stir fry, only rolling it in the liquids, and making sure not to break the crab meat.

Turn off the heat and add the holy basil leaves. Incorporate the basil leaves into the dish using only the residual heat: cooking the basil leaves will cause them to turn black, and will impair the flavor of the dish.

เนื้อปูผัดกะเพรา
neuua bpuu phat gra phrao

ผัดกะเพราหมูกรอบ

phat gra phrao muu graawp

STIR-FRIED CRISPY PORK BELLY WITH HOLY BASIL

INGREDIENTS:

250 gr crispy pork belly, sliced into bite-size pieces
(See page 98)
1 1/2 tablespoons garlic
1 1/2 tablespoon (or more) red and green bird's eye chilies
1 cup holy basil leaves
1 tablespoon natural taste oil

Season with:
1 tablespoon light soy sauce
1 tablespoon oyster sauce
1/4 teaspoon ground white pepper
pinch of salt
pinch of sugar
3 tablespoons stock or water

DIRECTIONS:

In a pestle and mortar, roughly crush the garlic. Add the bird's eye chilies and pound together until all the chilies are bruised; set aside.

Mix all the seasoning ingredients and set aside.

Place a well-seasoned wok over medium-high heat, and when the wok is hot, pour in the oil and then pour in the garlic and chilies mixture.

Sprinkle some water into the wok to deglaze it, then add the seasoning sauce.

Mix together and wait for the sauce to come to a boil, and add more water or stock as required.

Add the sliced crispy pork belly and quickly stir fry, only rolling it in the liquids.

Turn off the heat and add the holy basil leaves. Incorporate the basil leaves into the dish using only the residual heat: cooking the basil leaves will cause them to turn black, and will also impair the flavor of the dish.

ผัดกะเพราหมูกรอบ
phat gra phrao muu graawp

ผัดกะเพราตับไก่

phat gra phrao dtap gai

STIR-FRIED CHICKEN LIVERS WITH HOLY BASIL

INGREDIENTS:

200 gr chicken livers, sliced into bite-size pieces
1 1/2 tablespoons garlic
1 tablespoon (or more) red and green bird's eye chilies
1 cup holy basil leaves
1 tablespoon natural taste oil

Season with:
3/4 tablespoon light soy sauce
1 tablespoon oyster sauce
1/4 teaspoon ground white pepper
pinch of salt
pinch of sugar
1/3 cup stock or water

DIRECTIONS:

In a pestle and mortar, roughly crush the garlic. Add the bird's eye chilies and pound together until all the chilies are bruised; set aside.

Mix all the seasoning ingredients and set them aside.

Place a well-seasoned wok over medium-high heat, and when the wok is hot, pour in the oil followed by the garlic and chilies mixture. Stir fry quickly until fragrant; do not allow the garlic to brown.

Add the sliced chicken livers and quickly stir fry. Continue stir frying the livers until they are cooked to your liking.

Sprinkle some water to deglaze the wok, then add the seasoning sauce.

Mix together and wait for the sauce to come to a boil, then add more water or stock as required.

Turn off the heat and add the holy basil leaves. Incorporate the basil leaves into the dish using only the residual heat: cooking the basil leaves will cause them to turn black, and will also impair the flavor of the dish.

ผัดกะเพราตับไก่
phat gra phrao dtap gai

15

หมูทอดกระเทียมพริกไทย

muu thaawt gra thiiam phrik thai

FRIED PORK WITH GARLIC AND PEPPER

INGREDIENTS:

200 gr pork, sliced into thin bite-size pieces
1/4 cup Thai garlic
3 tablespoons natural taste oil frying

Marinate with:
1 tablespoon light soy sauce
1 teaspoon granulated sugar
1/4 teaspoon ground white pepper

Season with:
1/2 tablespoon fish sauce
1/2 teaspoon ground white pepper
pinch of sugar
pinch of salt

DIRECTIONS:

Mix and gently knead the pork with the marinade ingredients. Let rest for at least 20 minutes.

Mix all the seasoning ingredients; set aside.

Pound the garlic in a pestle and mortar. If using Thai garlic, leave the garlic unpeeled. Set aside.

Place a well-seasoned wok over medium-high heat. When the wok is hot, pour in the oil followed by the pork, and stir fry until the pork starts to caramelize.

Add the garlic and stir fry until the garlic becomes light golden.

Remove excess oil and add the seasoning mix. Stir fry together until all the liquids have evaporated, and the pork is coated evenly with the sauce.

หมูทอดกระเทียมพริกไทย
muu thaawt gra thiiam phrik thai

ไก่ผัดขิง

gai phat khing

STIR-FRIED CHICKEN WITH GINGER

INGREDIENTS:

200 gr chicken breast, cut into bite-size cubes
1/2 cup fresh ginger, thinly julienned
1/2 cup fresh black ear mushrooms
1/2 cup fresh banana chilies, cut into long, thin strips
1/3 cup large dry chilies, cut into 2 cm (0.8″) pieces
1 tablespoon garlic, crushed and roughly chopped
2 tablespoons natural taste oil

Season with:
1 tablespoon light soy sauce
1 tablespoon fermented soybean paste (*tao chiao*)
1/4 teaspoon ground white pepper
pinch of sugar
pinch of salt
1/3 cup stock or water

DIRECTIONS:

Mix all the seasoning ingredients; set aside.

Place a well-seasoned wok over medium-high heat. When the wok is hot, pour in the oil followed by the garlic. Stir fry quickly until fragrant; do not allow the garlic to brown.

Add the chicken breast meat; quickly stir fry until the chicken color has changed, then add the ginger and continue stir frying until the chicken is almost thoroughly cooked.

Sprinkle some water to deglaze the wok and create steam, and then add the black ear mushrooms and the fresh and the dry chilies.

Continue stir frying for a few more seconds before adding the seasoning sauce, then stir fry until the chicken is well done.

ไก่ผัดขิง
gai phat khing

19

ไก่ผัดเม็ดมะม่วงหิมพานต์

gai phat met ma muaang him ma phaan

STIR-FRIED CHICKEN WITH CASHEW NUTS

INGREDIENTS:

200 gr chicken breast, cut into bite-size cubes
1 tablespoon cassava flour or all-purpose flour
1/3 cup natural taste cooking oil

1 tablespoon garlic, crushed and roughly chopped
1/2 cup yellow onions, sliced into thin wedges
1/3 cup dry red chilies, fried and cut into 2.5 cm (1") pieces
1/2 cup raw cashew nuts
1/3 cup fresh long red chili peppers, thinly julienned
1/3 cup fresh banana chili peppers, cut into thin long strips
1/3 cup spring onions, cut into 2.5 (1") cm strips

Season with:
1 tablespoon light soy sauce
1/2 tablespoon dark soy sauce
1/2 tablespoon oyster sauce
1/4 teaspoon ground white pepper
pinch of salt
pinch of sugar
3 tablespoons stock or water

DIRECTIONS:

Mix all the seasoning ingredients. Set aside.

Roll the chicken cubes in flour. Remove any excess flour, and deep fry the chicken on medium-high heat until it turns light golden. Set the chicken aside on paper towels to absorb excess oil.

Fry the cashew nuts until light golden; set them aside on paper towels to absorb excess oil.

Fry the dry chilies until shiny and crispy; set aside on paper towels to absorb excess oil.

Wipe the wok clean with a paper towel, and place it back on the heat. Add about 1/2 tablespoon of oil and the garlic, and stir fry quickly until fragrant; do not allow the garlic to brown.

Add the sliced yellow onions, and stir fry until they become translucent.

Add fresh chilies and stir fry.

Sprinkle water to deglaze the wok and create steam, then add the seasoning sauce and stir fry until it thickens.

Add the fried chicken, along with the fried cashew nuts and fried dry chilies: toss all the ingredients together until everything is evenly coated with the sauce.

Add spring onions and stir fry; mix and serve.

ไก่ผัดเม็ดมะม่วงหิมพานต์
gai phat met ma muaang him ma phaan

เนื้อน้ำมันหอย

neuua naam man haawy

STIR-FRIED BEEF WITH OYSTER SAUCE

INGREDIENTS:

200 gr beef, sliced to thin bite-size pieces
1 tablespoon garlic, crushed and roughly chopped
2 tablespoons fresh red chili, cut into thin strips
1/3 cup spring onion, cut into 2.5 cm (1") pieces
1 tablespoon natural taste oil
3 tablespoons stock or water

Marinate with:
1/2 tablespoon light soy sauce
1 tablespoon cassava flour or all-purpose flour

Season with:
1 tablespoon oyster sauce
1/4 teaspoon ground white pepper
pinch of sugar
pinch of salt

DIRECTIONS:

Mix and gently knead the beef with the marinade ingredients, and let it rest for about 10 minutes.

Mix all the seasoning ingredients and set aside.

Place a well-seasoned wok over medium-high heat, and when the wok is hot, pour in the oil, and then the garlic.

Stir fry quickly until fragrant; do not allow the garlic to brown.

Add the beef and stir fry until the beef has just changed color, then add the seasoning ingredients.

Once the liquids are hot and have reached the desired consistency, add the fresh red chili strips and spring onion.

Turn off the heat and serve.

เนื้อผัดพริกสด

neuua phat phrik soht

STIR-FRIED BEEF WITH FRESH CHILIES AND YELLOW ONION

INGREDIENTS:

200 gr beef, sliced to thin bite-size pieces
3/4 tablespoon garlic, crushed and roughly chopped
1/2 cup fresh long red chili pepper, cut into thin strips
1/3 cup large fresh young green chili, cut into thin strips
1/2 cup yellow onion, sliced into thin wedges
1 tablespoon natural taste oil
1/3 cup stock or water

Marinate with:
1 tablespoon light soy sauce
1 tablespoon oyster sauce
1/4 teaspoon ground white pepper

DIRECTIONS:

Mix and kneed gently the beef with the marinade ingredients, let rest for about 10 minutes.

Place a well-seasoned wok over medium-high heat, when the wok is hot pour in the oil followed by the garlic. Stir-fry quickly until fragrant, do not allow the garlic to brown.

Add the beef and stir-fry until the beef has just changed color, add the sliced onion and stir-fry quickly before adding the stock or waters.

Once the liquids are hot and reached the desired consistency add the fresh chilies strips. Stir-fry quickly until the onions soften.

เนื้อผัดพริกสด
neuua phat phrik soht

ไก่ผัดเปรี้ยวหวาน

gai phat bpriaao waan

SOUR-SWEET STIR-FRIED CHICKEN

INGREDIENTS:

200 gr chicken breast, cut into bite-size cubes
1 tablespoon garlic, crushed and roughly chopped
1/3 cup fresh banana chili peppers, cut into thin long strips
1/2 cup yellow onion, sliced into thin wedges
1/2 cup red and yellow bell peppers, cut into large pieces
1/3 cup pineapple, cut into large pieces
1/2 cup tomatoes, cut into quarters
1/3 cup Thai cucumber, cut into large triangles
1/3 cup spring onions cut into 2.5 cm (1″) strips
1 tablespoon natural taste cooking oil

Season with:
1 1/2 tablespoons tomato ketchup
1 1/2 tablespoons granulated sugar
1 1/2 tablespoon 5% white vinegar
1 tablespoon fish sauce
pinch of salt
1/3 cup stock or water

DIRECTIONS:

Mix all the seasoning ingredients; set aside.

Place a well-seasoned wok over medium-high heat. When the wok is hot, pour in the oil followed by the garlic. Stir fry quickly until fragrant; do not allow the garlic to brown.

Add the chicken breast meat and quickly stir fry until the chicken color changes, then add the banana chili peppers, the yellow onion and bell peppers, and keep stir frying until the chicken is almost thoroughly cooked.

Sprinkle water to deglaze the wok and create steam, then add the pineapple, the tomatoes and the Thai cucumbers.

Continue stir frying for a few more seconds, and then add the seasoning sauce; stir fry until the chicken is well cooked.

Add the spring onions and stir fry until the sauce has thickened.

เนื้อผัดพริกไทยดำ

neuua phat phrik thai dam

STIR-FRIED BEEF WITH BLACK PEPPERCORNS

INGREDIENTS:

200 gr beef, sliced into thin bite-size pieces
1 1/2 tablespoons garlic, crushed and roughly chopped
1/2 cup red and yellow bell peppers, cut into large pieces
1/3 cup yellow onions, sliced into thin wedges
1/3 cup spring onions, cut into 2.5 (1″) cm strips
1 tablespoon natural taste cooking oil

Season with:
1 tablespoon oyster sauce
1/2 tablespoon light soy sauce
1/2 tablespoon Shaoxing Chinese cooking wine
1 tablespoon black peppercorns, roughly ground
1/2 tablespoon granulated sugar
pinch of salt
1/3 cup stock or water

DIRECTIONS:

Mix all the seasoning ingredients; set aside.

Prepare ice water in a spacious bowl and set it aside. Bring salt water to a strong boil. Blanch the red and yellow bell peppers for about 30 seconds in the salt water to soften them before transferring them to cool in the ice water bath. Once they have cooled, strain and set aside.

Place a well-seasoned wok over medium-high heat. When the wok is hot, pour in the oil followed by the garlic. Stir fry quickly until fragrant; do not allow the garlic to brown.

Add the beef and quickly stir fry until it just changes color, then add the blanched bell peppers, and keep stir frying until the beef is almost cooked.

Sprinkle water to deglaze the wok and create steam, then add the seasoning sauce; stir fry until the beef is cooked. Add the spring onions and stir fry until the sauce has thickened.

เนื้อผัดพริกไทยดำ
neuua phat phrik thai dam

ผักกาดขาวผัดหมู

phak gaat khaao phat muu

STIR-FRIED CHINESE CABBAGE WITH PORK

INGREDIENTS:

200 gr pork, sliced to thin bite-size pieces
3 cups Chinese cabbage, cut into large pieces
1/2 cup tomatoes, cut into quarters
1 1/2 tablespoons garlic, crushed and roughly chopped
1 tablespoon natural taste oil

Season with:
1 1/2 tablespoons light soy sauce
1/2 tablespoon oyster sauce
1/4 teaspoon ground white pepper
pinch of sugar
pinch of salt
3 tablespoons stock or water

DIRECTIONS:

Mix all the seasoning ingredients; set aside.

Place a well-seasoned wok over medium-high heat. When the wok is hot, pour in the oil followed by the garlic. Stir fry quickly until fragrant; do not allow the garlic to brown.

Add the pork and quickly stir fry until the pork is fully cooked.

Sprinkle water to deglaze the wok and create steam. Add the Chinese cabbage; stir fry until shiny.

Add the seasoning sauce and stir fry until the cabbage is almost soft.

Add the tomatoes and stir fry until the cabbage is cooked, and the tomatoes have softened.

ดอกกุยช่ายผัดตับไก่

daawk guy chaai phat dtap gai

STIR-FRIED CHICKEN LIVERS WITH FLOWERING CHIVES

INGREDIENTS:

150 gr chicken livers, cut into bite size pieces
3 cups flowering chives, cut into 4 cm (1.5″) long pieces
1 tablespoon garlic, crushed and roughly chopped
2 tablespoons natural taste oil

Season with:
1 tablespoon light soy sauce
1/2 tablespoon fermented soybean paste (*tao chiao*)
1/4 tablespoon oyster sauce
1/4 teaspoon ground white pepper
pinch of sugar
pinch of salt
1/3 cup stock or water

DIRECTIONS:

Mix all the seasoning ingredients; set aside.

Place a well-seasoned wok over medium-high heat, and when the wok is hot, pour in the oil and then the garlic Stir fry quickly until fragrant; do not allow the garlic to brown.

Add the minced chicken breast, and quickly stir fry until almost thoroughly cooked.

Sprinkle some water into the wok to deglaze it and create some steam.

Add the flowering chives, mix, and then sprinkle more water to create steam and help the cooking process.

When the chives are glossy, add the seasoning sauce and continue stir frying until done. Do not overcook - the chives should remain crunchy. Serve.

ดอกกุยช่ายผัดตับไก่
daawk guy chaai phat dtap gai

ตับเหล็ก

dtap lek

STIR-FRIED CHICKEN LIVERS, CHIANG-MAI LATE NIGHT-STYLE

INGREDIENTS:

200 gr chicken livers, sliced into bite-size pieces
1 tablespoon garlic, crushed and roughly chopped
1/3 cup spring onions, cut into 2.5 cm (1") pieces
1 tablespoon chili jam oil (See page page 102)

Season with:
1/2 tablespoon Chinese light soy sauce
1 tablespoon light soy sauce
1/2 tablespoon oyster sauce
1/2 tablespoon sesame oil
1/2 tablespoon dry chili flakes
1/2 tablespoon white sesame seeds, lightly roasted
2 teaspoons granulated sugar
pinch of salt
1/3 cup stock or water

DIRECTIONS:

Mix all the seasoning ingredients; set aside.

Place a well-seasoned wok over medium-high heat.

When the wok is hot, pour in the chili jam oil followed by the garlic. Stir fry quickly until fragrant; do not allow the garlic to brown.

Add the chicken livers and stir fry until well done.

Sprinkle some water to deglaze the wok and create steam. Add the seasoning sauce and continue stir frying until the sauce thickens.

Add the spring onion; stir fry for a few more seconds before transferring to a serving plate.

น่องไก่เล็กทอดผัดพริกแห้ง

naawng gai lek thaawt phat phrik haaeng

FRIED CHICKEN DRUMSTICK WITH DRY CHILI GLAZE

INGREDIENTS:

500 gr chicken drumsticks
natural taste oil for deep frying
1/2 cup kaffir lime leaves, torn
1/3 cup dry red chilies
1 tablespoon garlic, crushed and roughly chopped

Marinate with:
1 1/2 tablespoons light soy sauce
1/2 tablespoon oyster sauce
2 teaspoons ground white pepper
1 tablespoon sesame oil

Glaze with:
1 1/2 tablespoons oyster sauce
1 tablespoon light soy sauce
1 tablespoon palm sugar
1/2 tablespoon granulated sugar
1/2 tablespoon sesame oil
1/2 tablespoon Shaoxing Chinese cooking wine
1 teaspoon dark soy sauce

DIRECTIONS:

Mix and gently knead the chicken with the marinade ingredients, let it rest for about 1 hour.

Mix all the glazing ingredients; set aside.

Deep fry the chicken on medium-high heat until it turns a deep golden color. Remove the deep-fried chicken drumsticks and place them on paper towels to absorb excess oil.

Fry the kaffir lime leaves until crispy; place them on paper towels to absorb excess oil.

Fry the dry chilies until they are shiny and crispy, taking care not to burn them. Place them on paper towels to absorb excess oil.

Wipe the wok clean with a paper towel, and place it back on the heat. Add about 1 tablespoon of oil, along with the garlic. Stir fry quickly until fragrant; do not allow the garlic to brown.

Add the glazing sauce. Stir fry until the mixture bubbles and thickens.

Add the fried chicken drumsticks; toss them in the glaze until each one is evenly coated.

Add the fried kaffir lime leaves and fried dry chilies.

น่องไก่เล็กทอดผัดพริกแห้ง
naawng gai lek thaawt phat phrik haaeng

ผักบุ้งไฟแดง

phak boong fai daaeng

STIR-FRIED MORNING GLORY IN RED FLAME

INGREDIENTS:

4 cups morning glory, cut into 4-5 cm (1.5-2") pieces
2 tablespoons garlic, crushed and roughly chopped
2 bird's eye chilies, crushed
2 tablespoons natural taste oil

Season with:
1 tablespoon fermented soybean paste (tao chiao)
1/2 tablespoon light soy sauce
1/2 tablespoon oyster sauce
1/4 teaspoon ground white pepper
pinch of salt
1/3 cup stock or water

DIRECTIONS:

Wash and cut the morning glory into 4-5 cm (1.5-2") segments.

Place in a bowl and top with the crushed garlic, the bruised chilies and the seasonings: Do not mix!

Place a well-seasoned wok over very-high heat and add oil.

When the wok is screaming-hot and the oil starts to smoke, turn over the seasoned morning glory into the wok.

Be careful – it might ignite in a splash of hot flame.

If so, wait a few seconds for the wok to stop flaming, then start to stir fry. Mix quickly, and serve when the leaves have condensed but the stalks are still crunchy.

ผักบุ้งผัดกะปิใส่หมูสับ

phak boong phat gabpi sai muu sap

STIR-FRIED MORNING GLORY WITH MINCED PORK AND FERMENTED SHRIMP PASTE

INGREDIENTS:

100 gr minced pork
3 cups morning glory, cut into 4-5 cm (1.5-2") pieces
1 tablespoon natural taste cooking oil
1/3 cup stock or water

Chili paste:
1 tablespoon fresh bird's eye chilies
1/2 tablespoon Thai garlic, peeled
1 tablespoon shallots
1/2 tablespoon fermented shrimp paste (kapi)
pinch of salt

DIRECTIONS:

Wash and cut the morning glory into 4-5 cm (1.5-2") segments. Set them aside.

Using a mortar and pestle, pound the chili paste ingredients into a fine paste by pounding them one ingredient at a time, starting with the chilies and followed by the Thai garlic and the shallots. Add the fermented shrimp paste last. Set aside.

Place a well-seasoned wok over medium-high heat. When the wok is hot, pour in the oil followed by the chili paste. Stir fry quickly until fragrant.

Add the minced pork and stir fry, breaking down all the lumps. Continue stir frying the meat until all the liquids have completely evaporated, and the meat dries up and starts to brown.

Add the morning glory threads and stock. Continue stir frying until the morning glory is cooked but still crispy, and the sauce has thickened.

ผักบุ้งผัดกะปิใส่หมูสับ
phak boong phat gabpi sai muu sap

กะหล่ำปลีทอดน้ำปลา

galam bplee thaawt naam bplaa

STIR-FRIED CABBAGE WITH FISH SAUCE

INGREDIENTS:

4 cups green cabbage, cut into large pieces
2 tablespoons garlic, crushed and roughly chopped
3 tablespoons natural taste oil for frying

Season with:
1 tablespoon fish sauce
1/4 teaspoon ground white pepper
1/4 teaspoon sugar
3 tablespoons stock or water

DIRECTIONS:

Mix all the seasoning ingredients. Set aside.

Rinse the cabbage and dry it thoroughly. Place a well-seasoned wok over medium-high heat. When the wok is hot, pour in the oil for deep frying and fry the cabbage until it is soft.

Remove the cabbage from the oil and place on paper towels to remove excess oil. Set aside.

Remove the oil from the wok, but don't wash it, leaving it well oiled. Place the wok back over medium-high heat, and when the wok is hot, add the deep-fried cabbage along with the garlic.

Stir fry until the cabbage starts to caramelize; at this stage, pour in the seasoning mix and stir fry together until the cabbage is evenly coated with the sauce.

Place on a plate and serve.

ผัดแขนงปลาสละเค็ม

phat kha naaeng bplaa sala khem

STIR-FRIED BRUSSELS SPROUTS WITH SALTED QUEENFISH

INGREDIENTS:

2 1/2 cups Brussels sprouts
2 tablespoons salted queenfish (ปลาสละเค็ม)
2 tablespoons garlic, crushed and roughly chopped
2 tablespoons natural taste oil

Season with:
1/2 tablespoon light soy sauce
1/2 tablespoon fermented soybean paste (*tao chiao*)
1/4 tablespoon oyster sauce
1/4 teaspoon ground white pepper
pinch of sugar
1/3 cup stock or water

DIRECTIONS:

Rinse the salted queenfish in running water, and then soak it in water for 20 minutes to remove any excess saltiness; pat dry with paper towels.

Fry the fish over medium heat, skin side first, until it is evenly golden on all sides.

Remove excess oil, let the fish cool, and then crumble the meat with your fingers. Set aside.

Mix all the seasoning ingredients; set aside.

Prepare ice water in a spacious bowl and set it aside. Bring salt water to a strong boil. Blanch the Brussels sprouts for about 30 seconds in the salt water before transferring them to cool in the ice water bath.

Once they have cooled, cut off and discard the hard stems, and divide it into bite sizes pieces.

Place a well-seasoned wok over medium-high heat. When the wok is hot, pour in the oil and then the garlic. Stir fry quickly until fragrant; do not allow the garlic to brown.

Add the crumbled fish meat and stir fry quickly for few seconds. Sprinkle some water into the wok to deglaze it and create steam before adding the blanched Brussels sprouts. Quickly stir fry until the sprouts are glossy.

Add the seasoning sauce and continue stir frying until the Brussels sprouts are cooked. Do not overcook - the Brussels sprouts should remain crunchy. Serve.

ผัดแขนงปลาสละเค็ม
phat kha naaeng bplaa sala khem

บวบผัดไข่

buaap phat khai

STIR-FRIED LUFFA GOURDS WITH EGGS

INGREDIENTS:

3 cups luffa gourds, cut into triangle-shaped chunks
2 tablespoons garlic, crushed and roughly chopped
3 large eggs
3 tablespoons natural taste oil

Season with:
1 tablespoon fermented soybean paste (*tao chiao*)
1/2 tablespoon light soy sauce
1/2 tablespoon oyster sauce
1/4 teaspoon ground white pepper
pinch of sugar
pinch of salt
3 tablespoons cup stock or water

DIRECTIONS:

Cut the luffa gourds into triangle-shaped chunks (cut on the diagonal; then roll it a half turn and slice on the diagonal again. Repeat).

Mix all the seasoning ingredients; set aside.

Place a well-seasoned wok over medium-high heat. When the wok is hot, pour in the oil; when it starts to smoke, pour in the slightly beaten eggs. Scramble the eggs gently and allow them to cook only partially before transferring them to rest in a bowl.

Wipe the wok clean with a paper towel, and place it back on the heat. Add the garlic and stir fry quickly until fragrant; do not allow the garlic to brown.

Add the luffa gourd and stir fry while occasionally sprinkling water – this deglazes the wok and creates steam that will help cook the luffa.

When the luffa is fully cooked, and looks bright and transparent, add the seasoning sauce and stir fry until the sauce has thickened.

Add the partially cooked scrambled eggs, and gently mix them with the luffa, allowing it to set in nice chunks until the eggs are fully cooked and the sauce is at the desired consistency.

ฟักทองผัดไข่ใส่กุ้ง

fak thaawng phat khai sai goong

STIR-FRIED PUMPKIN WITH SHRIMP AND EGGS

INGREDIENTS:

200 gr medium size shrimp
1 1/2 cups pumpkin, diced into small cubes
1 1/2 tablespoons garlic, crushed and roughly chopped
2 large eggs
3 tablespoons natural taste oil

Season with:
1 tablespoon fermented soybean paste (*tao chiao*)
1/2 tablespoon light soy sauce
1/2 tablespoon oyster sauce
1/4 teaspoon ground white pepper
pinch of sugar
pinch of salt
2 tablespoons stock or water

DIRECTIONS:

Peel and devein the shrimp; set aside.

Bring water to a boil and cook the shrimp until it is half-way done. Cool in cold water, strain and set aside.

Mix all the seasoning ingredients; set aside.

Place a well-seasoned wok over medium-high heat. When the wok is hot, pour in the oil; when it starts to smoke, pour in the slightly beaten eggs. Scramble the eggs gently and allow them to cook only partially before transferring them to rest in a bowl.

Wipe the wok clean with a paper towel, and place it back on the heat. Add the garlic and stir fry quickly until fragrant; do not allow the garlic to brown.

Add the pumpkin, and stir fry while occasionally sprinkling water – this deglazes the wok and creates steam that will help cook the pumpkin.

When the pumpkin is fully cooked, and looks bright and transparent, add the seasoning sauce and keep stir frying until the sauce thickens.

Add the partially cooked shrimp and allow to fully cook.

Add the partially cooked scrambled eggs, and gently mix them with the pumpkin, allowing it to set in nice chunks.

Stir fry until the eggs are fully cooked and the sauce is at the desired consistency.

ฟักทองผัดไข่ใส่กุ้ง
fak thaawng phat khai sai goong

มะเขือยาวผัดเต้าเจี้ยว

ma kheuua yaao phat dtao jiaao

STIR-FRIED THAI LONG EGGPLANT WITH FERMENTED SOYBEAN PASTE AND THAI BASIL

INGREDIENTS:

4 cups Thai long eggplants, cut into triangle-shaped chunks
1 tablespoon garlic, crushed and roughly chopped
1 cup Thai sweet basil

Season with:
1 tablespoon fermented soybean paste (*tao chiao*)
1/2 tablespoon light soy sauce
1/2 teaspoon granulated sugar
3 tablespoons stock or water

DIRECTIONS:

Cut the eggplants into triangle-shaped chunks (cut on the diagonal, then roll the eggplant a half turn and slice on the diagonal again; repeat).

Mix all the seasoning ingredients. Set aside.

Boil the eggplant chunks in rapidly boiling water over high heat for about 3 minutes or until they soften. Strain and set aside.

Place a well-seasoned wok over medium-high heat. When the wok is hot, pour in the oil followed by the garlic. Stir fry quickly until fragrant; do not allow the garlic to brown.

Add the cooked eggplants along with the seasoning sauce, and stir fry only until the sauce is boiling.

Turn off the heat and add the Thai sweet basil leaves. Incorporate the basil leaves into the dish using only the residual heat: cooking the basil leaves will cause them to turn black, and will also impair the flavor of the dish.

ผัดถั่วงอกใส่เต้าหู้

phat thuaa ngaawk sai dtao huu

STIR-FRIED BEAN SPROUTS WITH FIRM TOFU

INGREDIENTS:

2/3 cups firm tofu, cut into 1.5 cm (0.6") cubes
1 1/2 cups bean sprouts
1 1/2 tablespoons garlic, crushed and roughly chopped
2 tablespoons natural taste oil

Season with:
1 tablespoon light soy sauce
1/2 tablespoon fermented soybean paste (*tao chiao*)
1/4 tablespoon oyster sauce
1/4 teaspoon ground white pepper
pinch of sugar
pinch of salt
3 tablespoons stock or water

DIRECTIONS:

Mix all the seasoning ingredients; set aside.

Place a well-seasoned wok over medium-high heat, and when the wok is hot, pour in the oil and then the tofu cubes. Fry until the tofu turns a light-golden color.

Add the garlic and stir fry quickly until fragrant; do not allow the garlic to brown.

Sprinkle some water into the wok to deglaze it and create some steam before adding the bean sprouts.

Quickly stir fry until the sprouts are glossy.

Add the seasoning sauce and continue stir frying until done. Do not overcook - the bean sprouts should remain crunchy. Serve.

ผัดถั่วงอกใส่เต้าหู้
phat thuaa ngaawk sai dtao huu

ผัดคะน้าน้ำมันหอย

phat kha naa naam man haawy

STIR-FRIED CHINESE KALE WITH OYSTER SAUCE

INGREDIENTS:

3 cups Chinese kale
1/2 tablespoon garlic, crushed and roughly chopped
1 tablespoon natural taste oil
2 tablespoons deep-fried crispy garlic

salt water for blanching
ice water for shock cooling

Season with:
1 tablespoon oyster sauce
1/2 tablespoon light soy sauce
pinch of salt
pinch of sugar
3 tablespoons stock or water

DIRECTIONS:

Mix all the seasoning ingredients and set aside.

Prepare ice water in a spacious bowl and set aside.

Bring salt water to a strong boil. Holding the Chinese kale by the leaf end, lower only the stems into the salt water, blanching for about a minute before submerging the entire leaf for an additional 30 seconds, and then transferring it to the ice water bath to cool.

This technique allows the woody part of the kale to cook longer than the green leafy parts; thus the kale is evenly cooked.

Once the kale has cooled down, transfer it to a cutting board, arranging all the leaves in the same direction. Cut the leaves into 4-5 cm (1.5-2″) segments without disturbing the layout. Transfer the kale into a serving plate, keeping the pattern intact.

Place a well-seasoned wok over medium-high heat. When the wok is hot, pour in the oil and then the garlic. Stir fry quickly until fragrant; do not allow the garlic to brown.

Add seasoning, and stir fry until the liquids have reached the desired consistency.

Pour the seasoning sauce over the blanched kale and sprinkle with deep-fried crispy garlic.

ผัดคะน้าน้ำมันหอย
phat kha naa naam man haawy

เห็ดผัดน้ำมันหอย

het phat naam man haawy

STIR-FRIED MUSHROOMS WITH OYSTER SAUCE

INGREDIENTS:

3 cups mixed selection of mushrooms (King Oyster, Shimeji and Bunapi mushrooms)
1 tablespoon garlic, crushed and roughly chopped
2 tablespoons fresh long red chili peppers, thinly julienned
1 tablespoon natural taste cooking oil

Season with:
1 1/2 tablespoons oyster sauce
1/2 tablespoon light soy sauce
1/4 teaspoon ground white pepper
pinch of sugar
pinch of salt
3 tablespoons stock or water

DIRECTIONS:

Mix all the seasoning ingredients; set aside.

Place a well-seasoned wok over medium-high heat. When the wok is hot, pour in the oil followed by the mushrooms.
Stir fry quickly until liquids start to render out of the mushrooms.

Add garlic and keep stir frying quickly; from time to time sprinkle water to deglaze the wok and create steam, until the mushrooms have softened.

Add the seasoning sauce and continue to stir fry until the sauce thickens.

Add the julienned red chilies and stir fry until the mushrooms are cooked.

ผัดเค็มเห็ดกระเทียม

phat khem het gra thiiam

STIR-FRIED MUSHROOMS WITH GARLIC AND SALT

INGREDIENTS:

3 cups mixed selection of mushrooms (King Oyster, Shimeji and Bunapi mushrooms)
1 1/2 tablespoons garlic, crushed and roughly chopped
1/3 cup spring onions, finely chopped
2 tablespoons dry bird's eye chilies, roasted and pounded
2 tablespoons dry bird's eye chilies, fried
1 teaspoon salt
1/2 tablespoon natural taste cooking oil

DIRECTIONS:

Roast the dry bird's eye chilies until charred, then pound roughly and set aside.

Place a well-seasoned wok over high heat. When the wok is hot, pour in the oil and let it heat up. Turn off the heat and add the dry chilies. Fry the dry chilies until they are shiny and crispy, taking care not to burn them. Cut the fried chilies into 1.5 cm (0.6″) pieces; set aside.

Remove the oil from the wok, but don't wash it – leave it well oiled. Return the wok to very high heat.

When the wok is hot, add the mushrooms. Stir fry quickly, and sprinkle water from time to time to deglaze the wok and create steam; repeat until the mushrooms have softened and all the liquids that render out of the mushrooms have dried.

Add garlic and stir fry quickly until fragrant.

Turn off the heat, and add the fried chilies, chopped spring onions and salt. Toss everything together and serve.

ผัดเค็มเห็ดกระเทียม
phat khem het gra thiiam

เห็ดหูหนูผัดผักกาดดอง

het huu nuu phat phak gaat daawng

STIR-FRIED BLACK JELLY FUNGUS WITH PICKLED CHINESE LETTUCE

INGREDIENTS:

2 cups fresh black ear mushrooms
1/2 cup pickled Chinese lettuce
1 tablespoon garlic, crushed and roughly chopped
natural taste cooking oil

Season with:
1 1/2 tablespoons light soy sauce
1/2 tablespoon sesame oil
1/4 teaspoon ground white pepper
pinch of sugar
pinch of salt
3 tablespoons stock or water

DIRECTIONS:

Mix all the seasoning ingredients; set aside.

Place a well-seasoned wok over medium-high heat. When the wok is hot, pour in the oil followed by the garlic. Stir fry quickly until fragrant; do not allow the garlic to brown.

Add the pickled Chinese lettuce, and quickly stir fry until it turns shiny.

Sprinkle water to deglaze the wok and create steam; add the black ear mushrooms, and continue stir frying for a few more seconds before adding the seasoning sauce.

Stir fry until the black ear mushrooms are cooked, but still crispy.

เห็ดหูหนูผัดผักกาดดอง
het huu nuu phat phak gaat daawng

ถั่วฝักยาวผัดเสฉวน

thuaa fak yaao phat saehchuaan

STIR-FRIED YARDLONG BEANS WITH DRY CHILIES AND SICHUAN PEPPER

INGREDIENTS:

2 cups yardlong beans, cut into 3.5 cm (1.5″) strips
1 tablespoon garlic, crushed and roughly chopped
1/2 tablespoon ginger, finely chopped
1 tablespoon preserved salted daikon radish
1/2 teaspoon Sichuan pepper, roughly ground
3 tablespoons dry red chilies
1/3 cup natural taste cooking oil

Season with:
1/2 tablespoon fermented soybean paste (*tao chiao*)
1 tablespoon light soy sauce
2 tablespoons stock or water

DIRECTIONS:

In a pestle and mortar, roughly pound the garlic and ginger; set aside.

Mix all the seasoning ingredients; set aside.

Place a well-seasoned wok over medium-high heat. When the wok is hot, pour in the oil and fry the yardlong beans until they look shiny and crispy. Remove the beans from the oil and place them on paper towels to remove excess oil. Set aside.

Fry the dry chilies until they're shiny and crispy, taking care not to burn them. Cut the fried chilies into 1.5 cm (0.6″) pieces; set aside.

Remove the oil from the wok, but don't wash it – leave it well oiled.

Return the wok to medium-high heat. When the wok is hot, add the garlic-ginger paste and stir fry until fragrant, then add the salted daikon radish and the seasoning mix.

Stir fry until the sauce thickens.

Add the fried yardlong beans, Sichuan pepper and fried dry red chilies: Mix quickly until the beans are well coated with the sauce.

ถั่วฝักยาวผัดเสฉวน
thuaa fak yaao phat saehchuaan

เห็ดหอมทอดซีอิ๊ว

het haawm thaawt see-iu

DEEP-FRIED SHIITAKE MUSHROOM STIR-FRIED WITH SOY SAUCE

INGREDIENTS:

3 cups fresh shiitake mushrooms
1 cup oil for deep frying
1 tablespoon Shaoxing Chinese cooking wine

Season with:
1/2 tablespoon light soy sauce
1/2 teaspoon sugar
1/4 teaspoon ground white pepper
1 tablespoon stock or water

DIRECTIONS:

Lightly rinse the mushrooms with cool water. Pat dry with paper towels, and remove the woody part of the stems.

Mix all the seasoning ingredients and set aside.

Place a well-seasoned wok over medium-high heat. When the wok is hot, pour in the oil for deep frying, and fry the mushrooms until they shrink. Remove them from the oil and place on paper towels to remove excess oil. Set aside.

Remove the oil from the wok, but don't wash it, leaving it well oiled. Place the wok back over medium-high heat.

When the wok is hot, add the deep-fried mushrooms and sprinkle Shaoxing Chinese cooking wine on the sides of the wok, followed by the seasoning sauce.

Stir fry until the mushrooms are evenly coated with the sauce. Place on a plate and serve.

กุ้งผัดพริกหยวก

goong phat phrik yuaak

STIR-FRIED SHRIMP WITH BANANA CHILI

INGREDIENTS:

250 gr medium size shrimp
1 1/2 tablespoons garlic, crushed and roughly chopped
2 tablespoons (or more) red and green bird's eye chilies
1 cup fresh banana chili peppers, cut into thin long strips
2 tablespoons pork fat or natural taste oil

Season with:
1 tablespoon fish sauce
1 tablespoon oyster sauce
2 teaspoons granulated sugar
pinch of salt
2 tablespoons stock or water

DIRECTIONS:

Peel and devein the shrimp, set-aside.

Mix all the seasoning ingredients and set-aside.

Peel and devein the shrimp; set aside. Place a well-seasoned wok over medium-high heat. When the wok is hot, pour in the oil and deep-fry the shrimp until the shrimp turns an orange color, or about 70% done.

Remove the shrimp from the wok, and set on paper towels to absorb excess oil.

Wipe the wok clean with a paper towel, and place it back on medium-low heat. When the wok is hot, pour in one tablespoon of oil followed by the crushed garlic and stir fry until fragrant; do not allow the garlic to brown.

Add bird's eye chilies, and stir fry until fragrant.

Add the banana chilies, and sprinkle some water to deglaze the wok and create steam.

When the banana chilies start to soften, increase the heat to high, and add the semi-cooked shrimp along with the seasoning sauce; continue stir frying until the sauce thickens and the shrimp are well cooked.

กุ้งผัดกระเทียมทรงเครื่อง

goong phat gra thiiam sohng khreuuang

STIR FRIED SHRIMP WITH GARLIC AND JEWELS

INGREDIENTS:

250 gr medium size shrimp
1 1/2 tablespoons garlic, crushed and roughly chopped
1/3 cup green onion, finely chopped
3 tablespoons shallots, sliced
2 tablespoons fresh long red chili peppers, diced into small pieces
2 tablespoons fresh yellow chilies, diced into small pieces
2 teaspoons black peppercorns, roughly ground
3 tablespoons spring onions, finely chopped
natural taste oil for deep frying

Season with:
1 tablespoon light soy sauce
1/2 tablespoon oyster sauce
pinch of salt
3 tablespoons cup stock or water

DIRECTIONS:

Peel and devein the shrimp; set aside.

Mix all the seasoning ingredients; set aside.

Place a well-seasoned wok over medium-high heat. When the wok is hot, pour in the oil and deep-fry the shrimp until the shrimp turns an orange color, or about 70% done.

Remove the shrimp from the wok, and set on paper towels to absorb excess oil.

Wipe the wok clean with a paper towel, and place it back on medium-low heat - do not add more oil. Add the garlic, and stir fry quickly until fragrant; do not allow the garlic to brown.

Add the shallots and diced fresh chilies, and stir fry quickly until the shallots start to soften.

Sprinkle some water to deglaze the wok and create steam; add the chopped spring onions and the black pepper, and mix well.

Increase the heat to high, and add the semi-cooked shrimp along with the seasoning sauce; continue stir frying until the sauce thickens and the shrimp are well cooked.

เนื้อปูผัดผงกะหรี่

neuua bpuu phat phohng garee

STIR-FRIED CRAB MEAT WITH CURRY POWDER AND EGGS

INGREDIENTS:

300 gr steamed crab meat
1 tablespoon garlic, crushed and roughly chopped
1/2 tablespoon ginger, finely chopped
1 teaspoon ground white peppercorns
1/4 cup fresh long red chili peppers, thinly julienned
1/3 cup spring onions, cut into 2.5 cm (1") strips
1 tablespoon chili jam oil (for garnish) (See page page 102)
2 tablespoons natural taste cooking oil

Season with:
1 1/2 tablespoons light soy sauce
1/2 tablespoon oyster sauce
2 teaspoons sesame oil
1 teaspoon granulated sugar
pinch of salt
2 tablespoons stock or water

Egg mix:
2 large eggs
1 tablespoon curry powder
1/4 cup evaporated milk
1 tablespoon chili jam (See page page 102)

DIRECTIONS:

Mix all the seasoning ingredients; set aside.

Mix all the egg mix ingredients; set aside.

In a pestle and mortar, pound the garlic, ginger and ground white peppercorns to a smooth paste.

Place a well-seasoned wok over medium-high heat. When the wok is hot, pour in the oil followed by the garlic-ginger paste. Stir fry quickly until fragrant.

Add the red chilies and spring onions, followed by the seasoning sauce.

When the seasoning sauce thickens, add the egg mix. Allow the egg mix to cook until the egg starts to form; gently scramble the eggs.

Add the crab meat and gently mix. Cook until almost dry, and drizzle the chili jam oil over it.

เนื้อปูผัดผงกะหรี่
neuua bpuu phat phohng garee

ปลาหมึกผัดกะปิ

bplaa meuk phat ga bpi

STIR-FRIED SQUID WITH FERMENTED SHRIMP PASTE

INGREDIENTS:

200 gr squid, cleaned, scored and cut into 2 cm (1″) strips
1 tablespoon fresh long red chili peppers, cut into thin strips
1/2 tablespoon kaffir lime leaves, very thinly (hair-thin) julienned
2 tablespoons natural taste cooking oil

Chili paste:
2 tablespoons fresh bird's eye chilies
1 1/2 tablespoons lemongrass
2 tablespoons Thai garlic
1 1/2 tablespoons shallots
1/4 teaspoon kaffir lime zest
1/2 tablespoon fermented shrimp paste (kapi)

Season with:
2 teaspoons palm sugar
2 teaspoons fish sauce
pinch of salt
3 tablespoons stock or water

DIRECTIONS:

Use a sharp knife to cut through one side of each squid lengthways. Open out flat with the inside surface facing up, and score crisscross patterns in the surface. Cut into 2 cm (0.8″) wide strips.

Bring water to a boil and cook the squid until it is halfway done. Cool in cold water, strain and set aside.

Using a pastel and mortar, pound the chili paste ingredients one by one, starting with the chilies and followed by the lemongrass, Thai garlic, shallots, kaffir lime zest; add the fermented shrimp paste at the end. Set aside.

Mix all the seasoning ingredients; set aside.

Place a well-seasoned wok over medium-high heat. When the wok is hot, pour in the oil followed by the chili paste.

Stir fry quickly until fragrant, and add water to dilute before adding the fresh red chilies.

Continue stir frying until the red chilies have softened, then add the squid and the seasoning sauce.

Keep stir frying until the sauce has thickened, and the squid is well cooked. Sprinkle the julienned kaffir lime leaves.

ปลาหมึกผัดกะปิ
bplaa meuk phat ga bpi

ปลาหมึกผัดน้ำพริกเผา

bplaa meuk phat naam phrik phao

STIR-FRIED SQUID WITH CHILI JAM

INGREDIENTS:

200 gr squid, cleaned, scored and cut into 2 cm (1″) strips
1 tablespoon garlic, crushed and roughly chopped
1/2 cup yellow onions, sliced into thin wedges
2 cups straw mushrooms, cut into halves
1/3 cup spring onions, cut into 2.5 cm (1″) pieces
1/3 cup fresh long red chili peppers, cut into thin strips

Season with:
1 tablespoon chili jam (See page 102)
2 teaspoons palm sugar
1 tablespoon light soy sauce
2 teaspoons oyster sauce
pinch of salt
3 tablespoons stock or water

DIRECTIONS:

Use a sharp knife to cut through one side of each squid lengthways. Open out flat with the inside surface facing up, and score crisscross patterns in the surface. Cut into 2 cm (0.8″) wide strips.

Bring water to a boil and cook the squid until it is halfway done. Cool in cold water, strain and set aside.

Mix all the seasoning ingredients; set aside.

Place a well-seasoned wok over medium-high heat. When the wok is hot, pour in the oil followed by the garlic. Stir fry quickly until fragrant; do not allow the garlic to brown.

Add the sliced yellow onions and stir fry until they are translucent, then add the straw mushrooms.

Sprinkle some water to deglaze the wok and create steam.

When the straw mushrooms start to soften, add the semi-cooked squid along with the seasoning sauce.

When the squid is nicely coated with the sauce, add the fresh red chilies and spring onions.

Continue stir frying until the squid and mushrooms are cooked.

ปลาหมึกผัดไข่เค็ม

bplaa meuk phat khai khem

STIR-FRIED SQUID WITH SALTED DUCK EGGS

INGREDIENTS:

200 gr squid, cleaned, scored and cut into 2 cm (1″) strips
1 large boiled salted duck egg
1 tablespoon garlic, crushed and roughly chopped
1/2 cup yellow onions, sliced into thin wedges
1/3 cup fresh long red chili peppers, thinly julienned
1/3 cup Chinese celery, roughly chopped
1/3 cup spring onions, cut into 2.5 cm (1″) strips
2 tablespoons natural taste cooking oil

Season with:
1/2 tablespoon oyster sauce
1/2 tablespoon light soy sauce
1/2 tablespoon granulated sugar
1/2 tablespoon commercial chili sauce, optional (Maggi or Heinz)
1/4 teaspoon ground white pepper
1/3 cup stock or water

DIRECTIONS:

Use a sharp knife to cut through one side of each squid lengthways. Open out flat with the inside surface facing up, and score crisscross patterns in the surface. Cut into 2 cm (0.8″) wide strips.

Bring water to a boil and cook the squid until it is halfway done. Cool in cold water, strain and set aside.

Mix all the seasoning ingredients; set aside.

Place a well-seasoned wok over medium-high heat. When the wok is hot, pour in the oil followed by the garlic. Stir fry quickly until fragrant; do not allow the garlic to brown.

Add the salted duck egg and stir fry until the egg yolk dissolves.

Sprinkle water to deglaze the wok and create steam. Add the yellow onions, and stir fry for about a minute or so, until the onions become transparent but not too soft.

Add the semi-cooked squid, along with the seasoning sauce.

When the squid is nicely coated with the sauce, add fresh red chilies and continue stir frying until the squid is fully cooked.

Add Chinese celery and spring onions; mix.

ปลาหมึกผัดไข่เค็ม
bplaa meuk phat khai khem

ปลากะพงปลาผัดคื่นช่าย

bplaa gra phohng phat kheuun chaai

DEEP-FRIED BARRAMUNDI STIR-FRIED WITH CHINESE CELERY AND FERMENTED SOYBEAN PASTE

INGREDIENTS:

250 gr barramundi, cut into 2.5 cm (1″) strips
cassava flour or all-purpose flour
natural taste oil for deep frying
1 tablespoon garlic, crushed and roughly chopped
2 tablespoons young ginger, thinly julienned
1/2 tablespoon Shaoxing Chinese cooking wine
1 tablespoon fresh long red chili peppers, cut into thin strips
1 tablespoon fresh yellow chilies, cut into thin strips
1/2 tablespoon fresh bird's eye chilies, roughly chopped
1 cup Chinese celery, cut into 2.5 cm (1″) pieces
1/3 cup spring onions, cut into 2.5 cm (1″) pieces

Season with:
1 tablespoon fermented soybean paste (*tao chiao*)
1/2 tablespoon oyster sauce
1/2 tablespoon light soy sauce
1/2 teaspoon granulated sugar
1/4 teaspoon ground white pepper
pinch of salt
3 tablespoons stock or water

DIRECTIONS:

Mix all the seasoning ingredients; set aside.

Cut the fish fillet into 2.5 cm (1″) strips. Roll the fish in the cassava flour, and remove any excess flour before deep-frying the fish.

Deep fry the fish on medium-high heat until it turns light golden. Remove the deep-fried fish strips and place them on paper towels to absorb excess oil.

Wipe the wok clean with a paper towel, and place it back on the heat.

Add about 1 tablespoon of oil, along with the garlic. Stir fry quickly until fragrant; do not allow the garlic to brown.

Add ginger, and continue stir frying until you can smell the ginger.

Add the Shaoxing Chinese cooking wine and stir fry until all the alcohol has evaporated.

Add the seasoning sauce. Stir fry until the mixture thickens, then add the fresh chilies and give them a few seconds to just slightly soften.

Add the spring onions and the Chinese celery, followed by the deep-fried fish. Gently mix the fish into the sauce until it is evenly glazed.

ปลากะพงปลาผัดคื่นช่าย
bplaa gra phohng phat kheuun chaai

ปลากะพงผัดพริกไทยดำกระเทียมโทนดอง

bplaa gra phohng phat phrik thai dam gra thiiam tho:hn daawng

DEEP-FRIED BARRAMUNDI STIR-FRIED WITH PICKLED ELEPHANT GARLIC AND BLACK PEPPER

INGREDIENTS:

250 gr barramundi, cut into 2.5 cm (1″) strips
cassava flour or all-purpose flour
natural taste oil for deep frying
1 cup pickled elephant garlic
1/2 tablespoon bird's eye chilies, bruised
1 tablespoon fresh yellow chilies, cut into thin strips
2 tablespoons deep-fried garlic
1/3 tablespoon black peppercorns, roughly ground
1/2 cup spring onions, cut into 2.5 (1″) cm strips
1/2 cup Chinese celery, cut into 2.5 cm (1″) pieces

Season with:
1 tablespoon light soy sauce
1 tablespoon oyster sauce
1 teaspoon black soy sauce
pinch of salt
3 tablespoons stock or water

DIRECTIONS:

Mix all the seasoning ingredients; set aside.

Cut the fish fillet into 2.5 cm (1″) strips. Roll the fish in the cassava flour, and remove any excess flour before deep-frying.

Deep fry the fish on medium-high heat until it turns light golden. Remove the deep-fried fish strips and place them on paper towels to absorb excess oil.

Wipe the wok clean with a paper towel, and place it back on the heat.

Add about 1 tablespoon of oil and the pickled elephant garlic; stir fry quickly until the pickled elephant garlic starts to caramelize.

Add the fresh bird's eye chilies and the yellow chilies; stir fry until fragrant.

Add the deep-fried garlic and the roughly ground black peppercorns, and continue stir frying for few seconds.

Add the seasoning sauce. Stir fry until the mixture thickens, then add the fresh chilies and give them a few seconds to just slightly soften.

Add the spring onions and the Chinese celery, followed by the deep-fried fish.

Gently mix the fish into the sauce until it is evenly glazed.

ปลากะพงผัดพริกไทยดำกระเทียมโทนดอง
bplaa gra phohng phat phrik thai dam gra thiiam tho:hn daaɯng

เนื้อผัดหน่อไม้

neuua phat naaw mai

STIR-FRIED BEEF WITH BAMBOO SHOOTS

INGREDIENTS:

200 gr beef, sliced into thin bite-size pieces
1 tablespoon garlic, crushed and roughly chopped
1 cup bamboo shoots, cooked and cut into long, thin strips
1 cup holy basil leaves
1 tablespoon natural taste oil
1/3 cup stock or water

Marinate with:
1 tablespoon light soy sauce
1 tablespoon oyster sauce
1/4 teaspoon ground white pepper

DIRECTIONS:

Mix and gently knead the beef with the marinade ingredients. Let it rest for about 10 minutes.

Place a well-seasoned wok over medium-high heat. When the wok is hot pour in the oil followed by the garlic.
Stir fry quickly until fragrant; do not allow the garlic to brown.

Add the beef, and stir fry until the beef just changes color.

Add the bamboo shoots, and stir fry quickly before adding the stock or water.

Once the liquids are hot and have reached the desired consistency, turn off the heat and add the holy basil leaves.

Incorporate the basil leaves into the dish using only the residual heat: cooking the basil leaves will cause them to turn black, and will impair the flavor of the dish.

เนื้อผัดหน่อไม้
neuua phat naaw mai

คอหมูผัดตะไคร้พริกไทยดำ

khaaw muu phat dta khrai phrik thai dam

STIR-FRIED PORK NECK WITH LEMONGRASS AND BLACK PEPPER

INGREDIENTS:

250 gr pork neck, sliced into thin bite-size pieces
1 tablespoon natural taste oil
1 teaspoon granulated sugar

Marinate with:
1 1/2 tablespoons light soy sauce
1 tablespoon oyster sauce

Lemongrass paste:
1/3 cup lemongrass
1/2 teaspoon salt
2 tablespoons garlic
1 tablespoon black peppercorns

DIRECTIONS:

Mix and gently knead the pork with the marinade ingredients. Let it rest for about 20 minutes.

In a pestle and mortar, pound the lemongrass with the salt into a smooth paste, then add the black peppercorns and garlic; pound together into a rough paste. Set aside.

Place a well-seasoned wok over medium-high heat; when the wok is hot, pour in the oil followed by pork. Keep stir frying the meat until any liquids evaporate completely, and the meat dries up and starts to brown.

Increase the heat and add the lemongrass paste. Stir fry until the paste is fragrant, then add sugar and stir fry until all the pork is coated with the paste.

คอหมูผัดตะไคร้พริกไทยดำ
khaaw muu phat dta khrai phrik thai dam

ผัดคั่วกลิ้งหมู

phat khuaa gling muu

STIR-FRIED MINCED PORK ROASTED CURRY, SOUTHERN THAI STYLE

INGREDIENTS:

300 gr minced pork
1 tablespoon natural taste oil
1/2 cup khua kling curry paste
1/3 cup kaffir lime leaves, very thinly (hair-thin) julienned
1/2 tablespoon fish sauce

Khua kling curry paste
1 1/2 tablespoons large dry red chilies, de-seeded
1/2 tablespoon dry bird's eye chilies
1/2 tablespoon ground white pepper
2 tablespoons lemongrass
1 tablespoon galangal
1 tablespoon turmeric
1 1/2 tablespoons garlic
1 teaspoon kaffir lime zest
1 tablespoon fermented shrimp paste (*kapi*)

DIRECTIONS:

In a pestle and mortar, pound the curry ingredients into a smooth paste, one by one in the order they are listed. Set aside.

Place a well-seasoned wok over medium heat. When the wok is hot, put in the *khua kling* curry paste, along with the minced pork.

Quickly stir fry, breaking down all the lumps.

Gradually the pork will render liquids. Stir fry until the meat is fully cooked and all the liquids have completely evaporated.

When the meat dries up, pour the fish sauce down the sides of the wok to create aromatic steam, mix well and turn off the heat.

Add the kaffir lime leaves. Incorporate the kaffir lime leaves into the dish using only the residual heat.

ผัดคั่วกลิ้งหมู
phat khuaa gling muu

หมูผัดเผ็ดกะทิสด

muu phat phet gathi soht

STIR-FRIED PORK WITH RED CURRY AND COCONUT CREAM

INGREDIENTS:

100 gr pork belly, sliced into thin bite-size pieces
100 gr pork meat, sliced into thin bite-size pieces
3 tablespoons fingerroot (krachai), thinly julienned
2 tablespoons fresh peppercorns
3 tablespoons kaffir lime leaves, hand torn
1/4 cup banana chili peppers, cut into thin long strips
1/4 cup fresh long red chili pepper, cut into thin strips
1/4 cup fresh yellow chilies, cut into thin strips
1/3 cup coconut cream
1/2 cup Thai sweet basil leaves
2 tablespoons natural taste oil

"*Phet*" curry paste: (1/2 cup)
1/3 cup large dry red chilies, de-seeded
1/2 teaspoon salt
2 tablespoons lemongrass
1 teaspoon coriander root
1 1/2 tablespoons galangal
1/2 teaspoons kaffir lime zest
1/4 cup Thai garlic
1/4 cup shallots
1/2 teaspoon coriander seeds, roasted and ground
1/2 teaspoon cumin seeds, roasted and ground
1/2 teaspoon white peppercorns
1 teaspoon fermented shrimp paste (*kapi*)

Season with:
1/2 tablespoon palm sugar
1 tablespoon fish sauce
1/3 cup stock or water

DIRECTIONS:

De-seed the dry red chilies and slice into small pieces, then soak in hot water until they have softened. Set aside.

In a pestle and mortar, pound the curry paste ingredients into a smooth paste, one by one in the order they are listed. Set aside.

Place a well-seasoned wok over medium heat. When the wok is hot, gradually pour in 3/4 of the coconut cream amount, stirring constantly until the cream separates and oil appears as small bubbles.

Add the curry paste. Stir fry quickly until fragrant; do not allow the paste to burn.

Add the pork. Stir fry the pork until it is thoroughly coated with the curry, and the meat is fully cooked.

Add the julienned fingerroot, fresh peppercorns and hand-torn kaffir lime leaves, and stir fry until fragrant.

Add the banana chili strips, along with the red and yellow chili strips.

Add the remaining coconut cream and the seasoning sauce, and cook until the sauce thickens.

Turn off the heat, and add the Thai sweet basil leaves.

Incorporate the basil leaves into the dish using only the residual heat: cooking the basil leaves will cause them to turn black, and will also impair the flavor of the dish.

หมูผัดเผ็ดกะทิสด
muu phat phet gathi soht

หมูผัดพริกแกงหน่อไม้

muu phat phrik gaaeng naaw mai

STIR-FRIED PORK WITH RED CURRY AND BAMBOO SHOOTS

INGREDIENTS:

250 gr pork neck, sliced into thin bite-size pieces
1 cup bamboo shoots, cooked and cut into long, thin strips
3 tablespoons kaffir lime leaves, hand torn
1 tablespoon natural taste oil

"Phet" curry paste: (1/2 cup)
1/3 cup large dry red chilies, de-seeded
1/2 teaspoon salt
2 tablespoons lemongrass
1 teaspoon coriander root
1 1/2 tablespoons galangal
1/2 teaspoons kaffir lime zest
1/4 cup Thai garlic
1/4 cup shallots
1/2 teaspoon coriander seeds, roasted and ground
1/2 teaspoon cumin seeds, roasted and ground
1/2 teaspoon white peppercorns
1 teaspoon fermented shrimp paste (*kapi*)

Season with:
1 tablespoon fish sauce
1 teaspoon palm sugar
1/3 cup stock or water

DIRECTIONS:

De-seed the dry red chilies and slice into small pieces, then soak in hot water until they have softened. Set aside.

In a pestle and mortar, pound the curry paste ingredients into a smooth paste, one by one in the order they are listed. Set aside.

Mix all the seasoning ingredients, and set them aside.

Place a well-seasoned wok over medium-high heat. When the wok is hot, pour in the oil followed by the curry paste. Stir fry quickly until fragrant; do not allow the paste to brown.

Add the pork and stir fry until fully cooked.

Add the bamboo shoots, and stir fry quickly until all the bamboo shoots are thoroughly coated with the curry sauce.

Add the seasoning ingredients and liquids, stir fry until the sauce thickens.

Add the hand-torn kaffir lime leaves, and turn off the heat.

หมูผัดพริกแกงหน่อไม้
muu phat phrik gaaeng naaw mai

หมูสามชั้นผัดพริกขิง

muu saam chan phat phrik khing

STIR-FRY PHRIK KHING CURRY WITH PORK BELLY AND YARDLONG BEANS

INGREDIENTS:

200 gr pork belly, cooked and sliced to thin bite-size pieces
2 tablespoons dried shrimp,
1/2 cup yardlong beans, cut into 1.5 cm (0.5″) strips
3 tablespoons kaffir lime leaves, hand torn
2 tablespoons natural taste oil

"*phrik khing*" curry paste: (1/2 cup):
1/3 cup large dry red chilies, de-seeded.
1/2 teaspoon salt
2 tablespoons lemongrass
1 teaspoon coriander root
1 1/2 tablespoons ginger
1 1/2 tablespoons galangal
1/2 teaspoon kaffir lime zest
1/4 cup Thai garlic
1/4 cup shallots
1/2 teaspoon white peppercorns
1 teaspoon fermented shrimp paste (*kapi*)
2 tablespoons dried shrimp, pounded

Season with:
1/2 tablespoon palm sugar
1 tablespoon fish sauce
1/2 cup stock or water

DIRECTIONS:

De-seed the dry red chilies and slice them into small pieces, then soak in hot water until they have softened. Set aside.

In a pestle and mortar, pound the curry paste ingredients into a smooth paste, one by one in the order they are listed. Set aside.

Rinse the dried shrimp, and dry in a dry wok over low heat. In a pestle and mortar, pound the dried shrimp until they become fluffy and soft.

Mix all the seasoning ingredients; set aside.

Place a well-seasoned wok over medium heat. When the wok is hot, pour in the oil followed by the curry paste. Stir fry quickly until fragrant; do not allow the paste to brown.

Add the fluffy dried shrimp, and stir fry until the mixture looks dry and a shiny red.

Add the pork; stir fry until fully cooked.

Add the yardlong beans, followed immediately by the seasoning sauce. Stir fry until the sauce thickens and the yardlong beans are shiny and crispy.

Add the hand-torn kaffir lime leaves and turn off the heat.

หมูสามชั้นผัดพริกขิง
muu saam chan phat phrik khing

93

เนื้อปูผัดพริกเหลือง

neuua bpuu phat phrik leuuang

STIR-FRIED CRAB MEAT IN SPICY YELLOW CHILI PASTE

INGREDIENTS:

300 gr steamed crab meat
2 tablespoons fresh yellow chilies, cut into thin strips
1/3 cup yardlong beans, cut into 1cm cm (1/2″) pieces
3 tablespoons kaffir lime leaves, hand torn
2 tablespoons natural taste oil

Chili paste:
1 tablespoon lemongrass
1/2 tablespoon galangal
2 teaspoons kaffir lime zest
1 tablespoon Thai garlic
1 tablespoon fresh red bird's eye chilies
1/3 cup fresh yellow chilies

Season with:
1 tablespoon fish sauce
1 teaspoons palm sugar
pinch of salt
1/3 cup stock or water

DIRECTIONS:

Prepare the chili paste: in a pestle and mortar, pound the lemongrass, galangal, Thai garlic, kaffir and lime zest into a fine paste; add the bird's eye chilies and fresh yellow chilies, and pound until all the chilies are bruised into a rough paste Set aside.

Mix all the seasoning ingredients and set them aside. Place a well-seasoned wok over medium-high heat. When the wok is hot, pour in the oil and then the chili paste. Stir fry until the paste is fragrant.

Add the yellow chili strips and yardlong beans; sprinkle some water into the wok to deglaze it.

When the beans are shiny and still crunchy, add the seasoning sauce. Mix together and wait for the sauce to come to a boil; add more water or stock as required.

Add the sliced steamed crab meat and quickly stir fry, only rolling it in the liquids, and making sure not to break the crab meat.

Add the hand-torn kaffir lime leaves; gently mix them in, and turn off the heat.

เนื้อปูผัดพริกเหลือง
neuua bpuu phat phrik leuuang

ปลาดุกฟูผัดขี้เมา

bplaa dook fuu phat khee mao

KEE MAO STYLE STIR FRY WITH FLUFFY CRISPY CATFISH

INGREDIENTS:

3 cups fluffy crispy fish
1 1/2 tablespoons garlic in large cloves
1 1/2 tablespoons (or more) red and green bird's eye chilies
2 tablespoons fresh yellow chilies, cut into thin strips
2 tablespoons fresh long red chili pepper, cut into thin strips
2 tablespoons fingerroot (krachai), thinly julienned
2 tablespoons fresh peppercorns
1/4 cup yardlong beans, thinly sliced
1/4 cup baby corn, thinly sliced
3 tablespoons kaffir lime leaves, hand torn
1 cup holy basil leaves
1 tablespoon natural taste oil

Season with:
1 tablespoon light soy sauce
3/4 tablespoon oyster sauce
1/4 teaspoon ground white pepper
pinch of salt
pinch of sugar
3 tablespoons stock or water

DIRECTIONS:

In a pestle and mortar, roughly crush the garlic. Add the bird's eye chilies; pound together until all the chilies are bruised. Set aside.

Mix all the seasoning ingredients; set aside.

Place a well-seasoned wok over medium-high heat. When the wok is hot, pour in the oil followed by the garlic and chilies mixture. Stir fry quickly until fragrant; do not allow the garlic to brown.

Add the strips of yellow and red chilies, along with the julienned fingerroot and fresh peppercorns. Stir fry until fragrant.

Add the seasoning sauce and mix. When the liquids are hot, add the sliced yardlong beans and baby corn. Continue stir frying until the sauce thickens, and the beans and corn are cooked - but still crunchy.

Add the fluffy crispy catfish; stir fry quickly until all the liquids have completely evaporated, and the fish dries up and is crispy.

Add the hand-torn kaffir lime leaves, turn off the heat and add the holy basil leaves. Incorporate the basil leaves into the dish using only the residual heat: cooking the basil leaves will cause them to turn black, and will also impair the flavor of the dish.

CRISPY PORK BELLY

INGREDIENTS:

300 gr pork belly
5% white vinegar
salt
1-2 stalks lemongrass, bruised
ground white pepper
natural taste oil for deep frying

DIRECTIONS:

Clean – Clean the pork belly thoroughly. Massage the skin side with salt and wash; repeat until the pork is clean, and dry it with a paper towel.

Marinate – In a tray that can fit the pork meat, dissolve about 1 tablespoon salt in 5% white vinegar, in an amount sufficient to cover only the thickness of the skin. Place the pork belly skin-side down in the vinegar solution; submerge, and let the skin marinate in the vinegar for 30 minutes. Wash and dry.

Cook – Cook the pork belly in boiling water with couple of bruised lemongrass stalks until it is just cooked. Dry and let cool.

Perforate the skin - Perforate the skin side multiple times using a fork or a designated tool available from Chinese cooking supply stores. Make sure to puncture only the skin.

Marinate – Place the pork belly in the vinegar solution skin-side down. Submerge and let the skin marinate in a new vinegar solution for 10 minutes. Then dry the pork with a paper towel.

Season – Sprinkle salt on both sides and rub it into the meat using your hands.

Dry – Heat an oven to 130°C (250°F). Place the pork belly in the oven skin-side up and allow it to dry. Turn it and dry it from all sides for about 1-2 hours.

Fry – Slice the pork belly into large chunks that fit comfortably in the wok. Fry in hot oil until it turns golden brown, and the skin is bubbled and nicely crisped.

หมูกรอบ
muu graawp

99

ปลาฟู

bplaa fuu

FLUFFY CRISPY FISH

INGREDIENTS:

4 cups grilled catfish meat
natural taste oil for deep frying

DIRECTIONS:

Using a cleaver-style knife, mince the fish meat on a cutting board. Chill in the fridge for about 10 minutes.

Remove from the fridge and in small batches, deep fry the fish meat in hot oil until it is golden and crispy.

Set the fried catfish on a kitchen towel to drain off any excess oil.

Grilled catfish meat can be substituted for any other oily fish meat that has been grilled or smoked until it's oily and dry.

ปลาฟู
bplaa fuu

น้ำพริกเผา

naam phrik phao

CHILI JAM

INGREDIENTS:

1 cup dry red chilies
1 cup shallots, sliced and deep fried
1 cup garlic, sliced and deep fried
1/2 cup dried shrimp, deep fried
natural taste oil for deep frying

Season with:
8 tablespoons palm sugar
6 tablespoons fish sauce
4 tablespoons tamarind paste
1 teaspoon salt

DIRECTIONS:

Prepare the ingredients. De-seed the chilies, rinse them and dry in a dry wok over low heat.
Rinse the dried shrimp, and dry in a dry wok over low heat.

Slice the shallots into thin slices; open the rinds, and spread on a kitchen towel. Pat dry using a paper towel. Set aside.

Slice the garlic into thin slices and spread on a kitchen towel. Pat dry using a paper towel. Set aside.

Deep fry all the ingredients until they become crispy, and golden in color. Start with the shallots, and then the garlic, followed by the dried shrimp. Turn off the heat, and fry the dry chilies using the residual heat.

When frying the shallots and garlic, be sure to remove them from the oil as they start to turn light golden; otherwise they will darken in color as they cool down.

In a pestle and mortar, pound all the deep-fried ingredients into a smooth paste. Set aside.

Place a well-seasoned wok over medium-high heat. When the wok is hot, pour in about a cup from the oil used to fry the ingredients, and then pour in the chili paste. Fry the paste until it is fragrant and add the seasoning mix. Allow the mixture to cool before storing it in a tight-lidded jar.

น้ำพริกเผา
naam phrik phao

103

Made in the USA
Lexington, KY
15 January 2019

6/28/24

i

Text: Dr. E. Aspler (Hanuman)
Images: Dr. E. Aspler (Hanuman), Noppadol Srinorakut (Ton)
ISBN: 9781521536629 (Print) ASIN: B072V2KY7D (Kindle Edition)
Thaifoodmaster.com